HYGGE

The Danish Art of Happiness
&
How to Hygge for Living a Cozy Life

By Steve Burgess

Table of Contents

1) What's Hygge? Everything you need to know about the Danish lifestyle

2) The Importance of Hygge in Denmark

3) 11 ways to make your Life more Hygge

4) Making your own Hygge Garden

5) Discovering True Danish Food

6) To discover this Delicious Cuisine & make it your Own

7) Hygge: Styling tips to achieve the Scandinavian look at Home

8) Ways to master the Danish art of Hygge in Your Home

9) Creating the Danish Hygge Look At Home

10) How to 'Hygge' your cosy log house Holiday

11) How to Create that Danish feeling that Danish feeling of 'Hygge' around the holidays

12) Why you need a 'Hygge' Family Holiday this Year

13) Top 5 Hygge Holidays

14) Embracing "Hygge" in the workplace

15) Ways to Use Hygge to get Cozy at work

16) Conclusions to Denmark's Happiness

What Is Hygge? Everything You Need To Know About The Danish Lifestyle

We're sure you've come across the word in the past few months, but what in the world is hygge exactly? First let's start with how you say it.

Pronounced "hoo-ga," this Danish concept cannot be translated to one single word but encompasses a feeling of cozy contentment and well-being through enjoying the simple things in life. If you've ever enjoyed reading a book indoors on a rainy Sunday or a cup of hot cocoa on a snow day you've experienced hygge without even knowing it. Hygge is such an important part of being Danish that it is considered "a defining feature of our cultural identity and an integral part of the national DNA," according to Meik Wiking, the CEO of the Happiness Research Institute in Copenhagen. "In other words, what freedom is to Americans. . . hygge is to Danes," Wiking says in his new book The Little Book Of Hygge, which comes out later this month in the U.S. This national obsession with all things cozy is credited as one of the reasons why Denmark is always at the top of the list of the world's happiest countries, despite their infamously miserable winters. Now the rest of the world is beginning to catch on to this wonderful way of life.

The basics. Similar to the German concept of gemütlichkeit and the Dutch idea of gezelligheid, the warm and cozy lifestyle that hygge promotes has been a key part of Danish culture since the early 1800s when the word first appeared in the written language (it's derived from a Norwegian word for "well-being"). While hygge—which is used as both a noun and adjective in Denmark—is more of a way of life for Danes, it caught on as a lifestyle trend in the UK in 2016 after several books about the topic were published. It became so popular in Britain that it was even included in the Collins Words of the Year for 2016—second only to Brexit. Now it's America's turn to go ga-ga for hygge. Everyone from The New York Times to The New Yorker has covered it and no fewer than eight books have been published in the last few months about the topic. It's trending on social media too. Pinterest predicted it will be one of the hottest home decor trends of 2017 after activity on the site about "hygge" increased 285 percent at the end of 2016. People have tagged over 1.5 million posts on Instagram with #hygge and have also taken to Twitter to discuss the finer points of what makes something hygge or not.

Yes, sweatpants count as hygge. There's even a word in Danish for them. Hyggebukser are that pair of pants you'd never be caught dead wearing in public, but practically live in when you're at home on the weekends binging on Netflix. In addition to describing things as hyggelig (hygge-like), Danes are also obsessed with adding hygge to other words to describe things. For example, a hyggekrog is essentially a nook where you can get cozy—imagine a window seat where you can wrap yourself up in a blanket and watch the world go by or your favorite armchair where you do all of your reading.

What other things are considered hygge? If you ask a Danish person, they're likely to tell you that candles are the most important part of creating a hyggelig atmosphere at home. Danes burn a whopping 13 pounds of candle wax a year per capita according to Wiking—more than any other country in the world. So turn off that unflattering overhead lamp and light some candles. Fireplaces, throw blankets, oversized sweaters and thick socks (really, anything knitted) also make things way more hygge.

What isn't hygge? Sorry, staring at your phone all day is the least hygge thing out there. TV is okay though—but try inviting some friends over to watch movies with you since togetherness is another key part of being hygge.

What about food? What you eat is also essential to creating those cozy vibes and it's all about homemade sweets, comfort food and hot drinks. While restaurants can certainly have a hygge atmosphere (think candles on the table and a fireplace in the back), spending tons of money on an expensive meal isn't the point. It's more about comfort and familiarity. In Denmark that might mean pastries, meatballs and copious amounts of coffee, but in America you might want to pour yourself a cup of hot cocoa, dig up your grandma's chicken pot pie recipe or spend a weekend afternoon baking your favorite chocolate cake.

Is hygge the next Marie Kondo? The trend seems to be going that way. While Marie Kondo's 2014 bestseller The Life-Changing Magic of Tidying Up inspired people to declutter their homes and only keep things that "sparked joy" in their life, hygge provides a friendlier and more forgiving lifestyle. While hygge is all about keeping things simple (think Scandi-style interior design), it also encourages people to live a little and say yes to that extra slice of cake. And after the divisive and stress-filled year that was 2016, it's no mystery why Americans are going all in for hygge in 2017.

So hygge = hibernating indoors alone all winter long? No, not exactly. While staying indoors all day long drinking hot chocolate and reading your favorite book alone is certainly hygge, getting outside to go for a long walk (yes, even in the winter) and spending time with friends and family is also a crucial part of the idea.

Can you make things hygge in the summer? Yes! While winter is the obvious time for all things hygge, Danes practice this concept year round. Some ideas forhyggelig summer activities include picnics in the park, backyard dinner parties, bonfires on the beach and outdoor movie nights.

Is this just a way to make us buy more stuff? At its heart, hygge is more about creating a certain atmosphere than things, so buying lots of expensive stuff is the opposite of hygge. But people are already starting to wonder if the UK and American versions of hygge are just an excuse for companies to sell people things (see The Guardian's "The Hygge Conspiracy" from last November).

So how do I make my life hygge without buying into the hype? If you want to read more about the idea, feel free to pick up any of the new books about it. But if you want to be truly hygge, just remember to appreciate the simple things that bring joy to your life. Instead of complaining about the bad weather this winter, light some candles and hunker down with a cup of tea and that book you've been meaning to read for months. Or if you're feeling more social, cook up a pot of your famous chili recipe and invite your friends over for a board game night. Have fun getting hygge with it!

The Year of Hygge, the Danish Obsession with Getting Cozy

"word of the year" shortlist was heavy on neologisms that one wishes didn't have to exist: "alt-right," "Brexiteer," and this year's winning term, "post-truth." Among the finalists, though, there was one bit of solace: "hygge," a Danish term defined as "a quality of cosiness and comfortable conviviality that engenders a feeling of contentment or well-being." Pronounced "hoo-guh," the word is said to have no direct translation in English, though "cozy" comes close. It derives from a sixteenth-century Norwegian term, hugga, meaning "to comfort" or "to console," which is related to the English word "hug." Associated with relaxation, indulgence, and gratitude, hygge has long been considered a part of the Danish national character. In a 1957 "Letter from Copenhagen" in The New Yorker, the writer Robert Shaplen reported that hygge was "ubiquitous" in the city: "The sidewalks are filled with smiling, hyggelige people, who keep lifting their hats to each other and who look at a stranger with an expression that indicates they wish they knew him well enough to lift their hats to him, too."

In the past year, this concept of Scandinavian coziness has made inroads with an international audience. At least six books about hygge were published in the United States this year, with more to come in 2017. (At the Guardian, Charlotte Higgins has done an investigation into the U.K.'s hygge publishing craze.) Helen Russell, a British journalist who wrote

"The Year of Living Danishly," defines the term as "taking pleasure in the presence of gentle, soothing things," like a freshly brewed cup of coffee and cashmere socks. Signe Johansen, in a cookbook and wellness guide, "How to Hygge: The Nordic Secrets to a Happy Life," links hygge to food and drink like cardamom buns, muesli "ne plus ultra," and triple cherry gløgg, a Scandinavian mulled wine with cardamom pods and star anise; she calls it "healthy hedonism." Louisa Thomsen Brits, the author of "The Book of Hygge: The Danish Art of Contentment, Comfort, and Connection," calls it "a practical way of creating sanctuary in the middle of very real life" and "a cure for SAD"—seasonal affective disorder—"in book form."

Winter is the most hygge time of year. It is candles, nubby woolens, shearling slippers, woven textiles, pastries, blond wood, sheepskin rugs, lattes with milk-foam hearts, and a warm fireplace. Hygge can be used as a noun, adjective, verb, or compound noun, like hyggebukser, otherwise known as that shlubby pair of pants you would never wear in public but secretly treasure. Hygge can be found in a bakery and in the dry heat of a sauna in winter, surrounded by your naked neighbors. It's wholesome and nourishing, like porridge; Danish doctors recommend "tea and hygge" as a cure for the common cold. It's possible to hygge alone, wrapped in a flannel blanket with a cup of tea, but the true expression of hygge is joining with loved ones in a relaxed and intimate atmosphere. In "The Little Book of Hygge," the best-selling of the current crop of books, Meik Wiking, the C.E.O. of a Copenhagen think tank called the Happiness Research Institute, shares a story about a Christmas Day spent with friends in a woodsy cabin. After a hike in the snow, the friends sat around the fireplace wearing sweaters and woolen socks, listening to the crackle of the fire, and enjoying mulled wine. One of his friends asked, "Could this be any more hygge?" Everyone nodded when one woman replied, "Yes, if a storm were raging outside."

Like many of the best things from Scandinavia, hygge might seem, to some Americans, to come with a whiff of smugness. The term is often mentioned in the same paragraph that reminds us that Danes (or, depending on the year, Norwegians and Swedes) are the happiest people in the world. Perhaps Scandinavians are better able to appreciate the small, hygge things in life because they already have all the big ones nailed down: free university education, social security, universal health care, efficient infrastructure, paid family leave, and at least a month of vacation a year. With those necessities secured, according to Wiking, Danes are free to become "aware of the decoupling between wealth and wellbeing."

"After our basic needs are met, more money doesn't lead to more happiness," he told Elle UK. "Instead, Danes are good at focusing on what brings them a better quality of life."

This vision of restrained pleasure harmonizes with a related Swedish concept, lagom, which refers to a kind of moderation. Pronounced with a hard "G," the term is said to come from the Viking phrase laget om, or "around the team," meaning that you should take only a sip of the mead that's being passed around so that no one is left without. Lagom means "adequate," "just right," or "in balance" and it is said to have burrowed deep into the Swedish national psyche, if not that of all Scandinavians. It encourages modesty and teamwork and discourages extremes. It is related to fairness, the need for consensus, and equality. Lagom is how a Swede might respond when someone asks how much milk you want in your tea or if things are going well. Hygge shares lagom's reverence for measured experience: indulging in a piece of cake, but not outright gluttony; a dinner with friends at home, but nothing fancy.

Some Scandinavians argue that lagom, instead of promoting virtues like humility and moderation, encourages the kind of bland conformity that Nordic countries are often accused of. In the 1933 novel "A Fugitive Crosses His Tracks," the Danish-

Norwegian author Aksel Sandemose wrote about the forced group mentality in a small fictional town called Jante. He lists ten soul-deadening rules by which the townspeople live, including "you are not to think you are special," "you are not to think you are good at anything," and "you are not to convince yourself that you are better than we are." In an article in T about his youthful dreams of fame, Karl Ove Knausgaard wrote about his own experience of what is known in Scandinavia as "the Law of Jante." As an adolescent in Norway, he wrote, "it didn't take much more than a slightly outlandish hat or a pair of unusual trousers before people told you off, laughed at you or, in the worst case, ignored you. 'He thinks he's special' was the worst thing anyone could say about you." Jante presents the more insidious side of lagom. Rather than celebrating modesty, it perceives individuality as a threat to the group. Robert Shaplen's "Letter from Copenhagen" quotes one Dane saying, "A foreigner shouldn't be too different from us if he wants to be liked. . . . We want everybody to be the way we are, because it gives us confidence in ourselves."

Louisa Thomsen Brits, a British-Danish writer, casts hygge as a state of mindfulness: how to make essential and mundane tasks dignified, joyful, and beautiful, how to live a life connected with loved ones. Her "Book of Hygge" focusses on the concept's philosophical and spiritual underpinnings rather than its quirky objects. She explains that many households in Denmark still have a copy of a folk songbook that they sing from to "affirm the ideas of simplicity, cheerfulness, reciprocity, community, and belonging." Danes, she says, prefer to gather in small groups "to emphasize the unity of their inner circles." She admits that this can make them appear "intimidating and impenetrable." These tendencies lend hygge its contradictions: what many see as humble, decent, and community-oriented may appear to others as insular and a rejection of what's different and unfamiliar. Scandinavia has a reputation for tolerance, but all three countries are tense over immigration these days and have seen surging support for far-right groups. Bo Lidegaard, a Danish historian, told the Times in September that many Danes feel strongly that "we are a multiethnic society . . . but we are not and should never become a multicultural society." Hygge encourages its practitioners to shelter, cluster, and enclose.

The most striking thing about hygge, though, might be how its proponents tend to take prosperity for granted. All the encouragements toward superior handicrafts and Scandinavian design, the accounts of daily fireside gatherings and freshly baked pastries assume a certain level of material wealth and an abundance of leisure time. As a life philosophy, hygge is unabashedly bourgeois, and American readers of a certain stripe will be familiar with its hallmark images—still-lifes of hands cradling a mug, candles lit at dusk on a picnic table, bikes with woven baskets and child safety seats leaning against a colorful brick wall. Artisanal this and homemade that, fetishizing what's rustic as authentic, what's simple as sophisticated: urban American sophisticates already know this aesthetic; we've aspired to it for a long time.

What many Americans do not aspire to is Scandinavia's high taxes or socialist ideas. When transferred to the United States, the kind of understated luxury that Danes consider a shared national trait starts to seem like little more than a symbol of economic status—the very thing that Scandinavian countries have sought to jettison. Still, there are some lessons from hygge that Americans might heed. There's the Nordic insistence on knowing how to do practical things and doing them well, on taking care of your body with time outdoors every day. The hard-earned lesson of frigid Scandinavian winters is that there's no such thing as bad weather, only unsuitable clothes—that all you really need to get through difficult times is shelter and sustenance, kith and kin.

The Importance of Hygge in Denmark

Georgsen explains: 'Hygge is not a thing or something you buy, hygge is a state of mind. You can have hygge on your own or with family and friends. It relates to a certain atmosphere. Sometimes you have tried to create the right environment for hygge, maybe lighting the fireplace, music, selected wine etc., but hygge will not just appear if your mindset is not ready and the interaction with people on that specific occasion is not happening. You simply cannot dictate hygge to just come around when you need it.

'To a large degree, Danes create their homes to reflect hygge,' he continues. 'This does not mean white romantic furniture with ornaments or flowered sofa textiles and wallpaper in pink. They create a home that radiates "I love to live here" and "I have a history, family, friends", and "I feel at home here and please come and feel at home together with me".'

Georgsen concludes: 'We Danes love the state of mind - hygge - because it's peaceful, friendly and a fantastic stress reliever. It's our zen, we breath it, almost live from it. Maybe it's one of the reasons that the Danes year in, year out are nominated the happiest people in the world.'

11 Ways to Make Your Life More Hygge

Although there is no literal translation, hygge (pronounced hoo-ga) alludes to a feeling of cozy intimacy and contentment. It's all about creating feelings of happiness, friendliness and wellbeing within everyday life.

It's about finding deeper meaning within ordinary life and establishing a meaningful, mindful connection with the world. Hygge is not about grand gestures, but rather, embracing little luxuries everyday in order to foster a sense of familiarity, comfort and kinship. How lovely.

So, as the darker evenings draw in, it's time to hunker down, settle in and do as the Danes do. Here's how:

1. Spend quality time with friends and family.

We all know that having a good time with people we love makes us happy. But when was the last time you sat around a big table with all of your nearest and dearest and shared stories until the wee hours? Laughing, joking and drinking homemade apple cider—this is hygge.

2. Sit by a roaring log fire.

Few things evoke feelings of coziness and warmth more than a roaring fire during the coldest months. A proper "hyggeligt" (translate: cozy) fire should, of course, use real wood. In fact, a real hyggeligt living room should certainly have its own log pile.

3. Keep things simple.

Why spend hours cooped up in the kitchen, agonizing over recipe books to create complicated dishes. Do things the Danish way and keep the food simple, whether that be a heart-warming soup or simple roast chicken, always opt for something delicious that can be cooked with minimum fuss.

4. Dim the lights and use candles instead.

Danes love candles, and so do we. The flickering flames create an ephemeral glow and add a brooding sense of atmosphere to even the darkest room. But be warned, never go for the scented kind. Nothing about hygge is artificial – not even the candles. Beeswax is best.

5. Decorate the inside with the outside.

Here at Country Living, we believe a happy, healthy life is one lived within nature. But sometimes it's just too chilly to go outside. To counteract this, Danes are big fans of bringing the outdoors inside: Think exposed stone walls, wooden floors, huge tables made from great trees and, of course, big piles of logs ready to be thrown on a roaring open fire.

6. Bake bread.

The smell of a freshly baked rustic loaf wafting through the house is about as hygge is it gets. Kneading the dough can be very cathartic and tucking into a home-made bake, straight from the oven, with family and friends, is one of life's great simple pleasures.

7. Drink cocoa.

Preferably stirred slowly over a hot stove and made using fine, real chocolate, cream and milk, then poured into big mugs and consumed in your cozy living room with friends. Mmmm delicious.

8. Don't deprive yourself.

Hygge is all about indulging in the good things in life, the things that make us truly happy – which, yes, often means eating cake and pastry. Well, we don't mind if we do!

9. Get outside.

There's more to hygge than staying cooped up indoors. You see, it's all about balance and living a good, healthy life – so exposure to nature is absolutely key. Going for a wellie walk wearing a warm scarf with the wind whipping up your hair – that's 100% hygge too (so long as you dive straight back to the sofa afterwards to enjoy a cup of cocoa).

10 Things Every House in the Country Needs

Although hygge encompasses a feeling of familiarity and togetherness, you can still achieve it alone. There are few things more hygge than cuddling up under a blanket and getting sucked into a proper, paper book – rather than the electronic kind. Is there anything more exquisite than that new book smell?

11. Put down the iPhone.

Hygge is the antidote to modern life. It's all about embracing these experiences fully and living in the moment, which is difficult to do when staring at a teeny weeny screen. So put down the phone and enjoy the feeling!

Making Your Own Hygge Garden

Winter is on its way. The temperature is dropping, the days are getting shorter and darker, and the temptation to give in to seasonal sadness is growing. But wait just a moment—this is where hygge comes in. Garden designer Caroline Tilston explains how you can apply it to your garden...

Hygge (pronounced hoo-gah) is a wonderful Danish lifestyle concept that revolves around happiness and taking pleasure in the small things. The freshly brewed coffee in your favorite mug, an arrangement of beautiful flowers on the table, special friends over for a lovely meal, and the beauty of a scented candle — these are all things we should relish. In fact, Danes use up more candles per head of population than anywhere else in Europe.

Hygge is quite a deliberate, self-conscious thing, too. What will this feel like? Will this create a great memory? It's all about noticing and being grateful for whatever we can be and making every moment as good as it can be. Rather like practicing mindfulness.

The overall message is that the source of happiness is not about material goods and not about buying stuff, but about rich and meaningful experiences.

So how can we translate this art of living Danishly into our gardens? In many ways it's easier to add hygge to your garden than to your house as there's more room to experiment. There are so many ways you can enjoy your garden in the winter: the views, the scents and experiences...

1. Get cozy

Cosy up around the fire outside. Most of us don't have fireplaces inside the house so it's a real treat to bring an open fire into the garden and it's so much easier out there. All it takes is a firepit, firebowl or kadai. Add in some logs or charcoal, and for treats supply some sticks, marshmallows, biscuits and chocolate to make s'mores. Invite friends over and you have a perfect hygge moment.

2. Embrace the view from inside

It's not always possible to get out into the garden in the depths of winter so think about the views you get from inside. Each view can be looked on as a picture with its own frame. Look at the view from each room to see what can be brought in to give it focus, then add some color and make it work. And every time you glimpse the garden now it will be that little bit more special.

3. Make the small details count

As well as the big views, focus in on the details: a terracotta pot planted with violas or pansies on the table, or a sculpture in amongst the plants. It takes a little bit of effort to keep it looking just so, but it's worth it for the everyday pleasure.

4. Introduce winter-scented flowers

Scents are all part of the feel-good movement, and in the garden it's a lot easier to introduce some wonderful smells, even in winter. Try winter-flowering honeysuckle (Lonicera fragrantissima) which will climb over fences or around doorways. Not a climber but good to grow against a wall, wintersweet (Chimonanthus praecox), is a deciduous shrub with amazing winter-scented flowers.

5. Don't forget the candles

It's possible to have a wealth of candles outside, but warm, white outdoor fairy lights can recreate the candle magic and are a lot easier to light. String them overhead for a star light effect or thread them through the planting to make the whole place hum with contentment.

6. Find new ways to enjoy the outdoors

On those cold, clear winter nights, take out blankets to watch the stars or the sunrise. Wrap up and provide hot water bottles for extra warmth and create a unique memory. Go one step further down the hygge highway and put in a hot tub and sauna for the full Scandinavian experience.

7. Make the most of the winter sun

Look at where the winter sun hits your garden and place a seat to catch it. Your morning coffee will be transformed if you can soak up winter light. And don't forget a seat in the sun is a wonderful thing to look at even if you never sit in it; just the possibility of sitting there will lift your spirits.

Discovering True Danish Food

went to Copenhagen for the first time in September, and ever since, I've been in love with Danish food. It's good for you; it's fresh and unique, and it's actually surprisingly easy to prepare at home.

Danish food is one of four Scandinavian or Nordic cuisines, along with Norwegian, Swedish, and Finnish. Given the geography of Scandinavia, it's perhaps no surprise that all of these cuisines heavily feature fish, seafood, and game. Many traditional dishes also play up the tradition of jarring, pickling, or otherwise putting up foods, due to the long winters in the region.

The Nordic diet, which is rich in berries, fatty fish, whole grains, and root vegetables was also recently identified by a study published in the European Journal of Internal Medicine as being a great healthy alternative for people with metabolic syndrome.

Danish food has a few specific characteristics as well. It features quite a lot of brassicas, rye, fish, pork, and potatoes, and dairy cooperatives developed in the second half of the 19th century increased consumption of milk and cheese, bringing cheeses like Danish blue and fermented milk products like ymer to this culinary landscape.

Breakfasts in Denmark tend to be simple, comprised of bread, butter, and cheese, or ymer topped either with muesli or ymerdrys, a mixture of grated rye bread and brown sugar. Special occasion or weekend breakfasts may also feature rye bread porridge or wienerbrød (Vienna bread), also known as Danishes.

Lunches and dinners feature a good deal of local produce, and they also tend to effortlessly blend sweet and savory, with a good deal of pickles and slightly sweet sauces paired with savory meats and fish.

The popularity Danish grainy rye bread, as well as sausage and other cured meats, contributed to the development of smørrebrød, the traditional Danish open-faced sandwich that remains a staple of Danish meals to this day. While the term comes from the Danish smør og brød, meaning "butter and bread," smørrebrød often consists of several ingredients, including cold cuts, liver paste, smoked or pickled fish, or cheese, all of which are piled on top of a slice of buttered rye bread.

Today, restaurants serve pre-assembled smørrebrød, which are often beautiful works of art. At home, however, the tradition is to put out a "cold buffet" (the Danish counterpart of the Swedish smorgasbord), allowing each individual to assemble his or her own sandwich.

Today, Danish food is also at the forefront of culinary modernity, with chefs like René Redzepi of Noma renewing and revisiting classic dishes and produce and inspiring cuisine worldwide. Restaurants in Copenhagen, especially, feature innovative dishes that approach traditional Danish cuisine in exciting new ways.

To discover this delicious cuisine and make it your own

Here are a few Danish recipes to try at home.

1.Danish Rye Bread

Danish rye is a grainy bread that is the staple of many Danish dishes – it's probably the best place to start if you're going to be making Danish food at home. Thin slices of the bread are used as the base of smørrebrød, and leftover pieces or stale crumbs are often made into porridge or toasted and sprinkled on top of both savory and sweet dishes.

2. Egg Salad with Salmon

Salads with mayonnaise-based dressings are quite common in Denmark, like this boiled egg salad, made with smoked salmon, capers, red onion, and dill. Eat it plain or pile it on top of a slice of Danish rye for a simple, delicious smørrebrød

3. "Italian" Salad

Perhaps the most common mayonnaise-based salad in Denmark is known as "Italian" salad. This salad – which is unlike any salad you'd likely find in Italy – is made with carrots, asparagus, peas, and a touch of mustard. In fact, some say that its name comes from its use of the colors of the Italian flag. It's commonly served on smørrebrød with ham or beef tongue

4. Cured Salmon Salad

Cured salmon is common throughout Scandinavia; this salad combines gravadlax, cured with dill and juniper berries, with beetroot, a local favorite that's easy to come by in Denmark and adds a touch of sweetness to the dish

5. Fish Cakes

Fish cakes or frikadeller are an easy-to-make dinner. In Denmark, they're commonly served with Danish remoulade, made with homemade mayonnaise, capers, pickles, tarragon, and a touch of curry powder.

6. Beetroot Salad

This dish is commonly found on Christmas tables, but it's easy enough – and delicious enough – to enjoy year-round. Pickled beetroot is combined with apple, mayonnaise, and crème fraiche for a sweet and creamy salad.

7. Pork Roast

Pork roast may not seem uniquely Danish, but the Danes really know how to make it right. In Denmark, the rind is always left on the pork, so that as it cooks, it turns crispy (and keeps the meat moist). To prepare this dish, be sure to ask your butcher to leave the rind on the roast, and then follow the instructions for scoring the fat and ending up with lovely slices that are easy to serve.

8. Danish Cinnamon Twist

The breakfast item that we know as a Danish actually has several iterations in Denmark. The kanelstang is one popular version: this pastry translates to "cinnamon rod" and is made by layering a yeast dough with a cinnamon and brown sugar filling. The rod is topped with a sweet icing and chopped hazelnuts.

9.Summer Soup

This sweet soup is made with your choice of cultured dairy, like buttermilk, kefir, or yogurt, which is sweetened with dates. The soup is served with seasonal fruit, rye breadcrumbs, or cookies, depending on your preference. It's also easy to make with oat milk and vegan yogurt.

10 .Norwegian Boller:

To a Norwegian, there's nothing better than fresh baked bread. Butter up one of these hot Norsk bollers straight out of the oven and bring on the warm fuzzies.

11.Deliciously Vegan Swedish Cinnamon Rolls:

Coffee and kanellbular are one of the absolute pleasures of Sweden and a great way to start your day. Ask a friend to join you and it turns into a fika — a coffee break and social celebration that springs up any time a friend drops by

12.Peaches and Cream Ebleskivers:

the morning off right with some light and fluffy ebelskiver — a cross between a pancake and a popover. Apples would be more traditional than peaches, but you can use whatever fruit you have on hand and they'll taste absolutely divine with a plop of whipped cream

13.Øllebrød (Danish Rye Bread Porridge)

Move over, oatmeal; this isn't your average breakfast porridge — unless it's your habit to have Guinness in your cereal. Made of soaked day-old rye bread that's sweetened with honey and citrus peel along with raisins and spices, it tastes SO yummy that it may quickly become your brekkie go-to

14.Smorrebrod With Egg, Avocado and Radish:

Long before the avocado trend hit Instagram, there was smørrebrød, loosely translated as "things on toast." Top yours with salmon, cucumber, dill or whatever tidbits of food you have on hand, and it will be absolutely spot on

15.Pumpkin Soup With Orange and Parmigiano-Reggiano :

Scandinavian cooking is full of hearty, creamy soups that are perfect for lunch but could also stand in for supper. This wintry soup, made of sweet, caramelized roasted pumpkin, is sure to raise your spirits as it warms your belly.

16. Danish Split Pea Soup With Dill:

If you thought you knew pea soup, prepare to be blown away by this tasty vegan version. The added brightness of dill and richness of crispy onions will make it your go-to soup this winter.

17. Nordic Roasted Cauliflower Soup:

Soup is always cozy, warming your whole body as it goes down. Just the pleasure of holding a spoon to your lips and blowing off rising swirls of steam slows your pace and creates a moment of restful pleasure. This version has a subtle hint of cardamom that you will utterly savor

18. Rømmegrøt (Milk and Flour Porridge):

This porridge calls for an ocean of melted butter and cinnamon-sugar on top. It's often eaten for breakfast Christmas morning, but it makes an awesome belly warmer after a cold afternoon spent playing in the snow.

19.Danish Roasted Pork:

Flæskesteg is one of Denmark's hallmark dishes and is often served at Christmas dinner. Be sure to nab a slice with lots of fatty crackling, so you can savor its sheer crispy pork perfection.

20.. Sliced Baked Potato (Hasselback) With Rosemary and Gruyere:

These Hasselback potatoes are sliced super thin and brushed with butter, then tiny slices of aged Gruyere cheese are slipped into every crevice. Oh, em, gee — it's like comfort food on steroids.

21. Norwegian Potato Dumplings (Potato Klub):

These dumplings are hiding a tasty little nugget of pork, herbs and onion. Eat yours in one bite to taste ALL the flavors at once and you'll be in hygge heaven.

22. Seriously Amazing Swedish Meatballs in Brown Gravy:

These little meatballs are just like IKEA's, only homemade. They're simmered in a creamy brown gravy that's SOOOOO good you'll wanna slurp it through a straw.

23. Seafood Stew:

These smell of this seafood stew as it simmers on the stove will bring back every outing you've ever had to the sea. Tear into the rustic bread, dip a piece in the creamy white wine sauce and let the juice dribble down your chin

24. Gluten Free Lefse:

The one's for the GF peeps in the house! Potato flatbread is a Norwegian holiday treat that's usually topped with butter and sugar, but this one tastes just as delicious slathered in ghee and honey.

25. Mulled Red Wine Jelly:

This mulled red wine jelly is full of holiday spices like cinnamon, bay leaves and orange peel. It tastes great on bread, but is equally good as a conserve on grilled cheese sandwiches, burgers, baked chicken or even vanilla ice cream

26. Risalamande – Danish Rice Dessert for Christmas:

Risalamande is traditionally served for dessert after Christmas dinner, but it's delicious any time of year. It's naturally gluten-free, so invite your GF peeps to share and you'll be their BFF.

27. Rosette Cookies:

These delicate rosette cookies called struva are a Christmas tradition in Norway and Sweden, and boy are they GOOOOD! You'd better make a double batch, because cookies this light, crisp and buttery are sure to go fast.

28.. Norwegian Apple Cake:

Apple cake is to Norway as apple pie is to America. Bake yours on a chilly morning while you loaf around in woolen socks with a flannel blanket over your shoulders and a huge cup of hot tea in your hands. It will be a hygge glut on all your senses.

29.Blackberry Glögg:

Mulled wine is a Nordic tradition and is almost mandatory in December, lending its warm comfort to shoppers in outdoor Christmas markets everywhere. It tastes just like an intensely spiced warm lemonade spiked with wine and rum. Wine lushes FTW

30. Aquavit & Rosemary Cocktail:

Every aquavit cocktail is a nod to Norwegian tradition. This one, sweetened with homemade rosemary syrup and garnished with a sprig of herb and twist of orange peel, looks so festive and it goes down REAAAAL easy

Hygge: Styling tips to achieve the Scandinavian look at home

1. MAKE SURE YOUR HOME IS WARM AND COMFY

It's very hard to feel hygge if you freeze, sweat or are uncomfortable. So the indoor environment is the foundation. Also make sure your home has good acoustics - bad acoustics make people talk louder and listen less and creates an anti hygge environment

2. DON'T MAKE YOUR HOME LIKE A PAGE IN A MAGAZINE

Make the hygge that fits you! Go to some Scandinavian design blogs or to BoConcept.com and get inspired by pictures. Scandinavian furniture, lighting and accessories are a good way to start. If you feel you are stocked, ask an interior designer to help you following the inspirational pics you have found. Wood finishes like warm walnut and natural oak never fail

3. YOUR PAST IS A BIG PART OF HYGGE

Books, LPs, heritage pieces etc., mix them with Scandinavian furniture. The merit with Danish furniture is that it is almost anonymous without been boring, which makes it easier to mix and match and create hygge

4. LESS IS (MUCH) MORE

These are words echoed by Mies Van der Rohe, and they are the absolute key words when creating hygge. If you have a small living room, use small nesting tables instead of a huge coffee table - it also makes it easy for you to create various atmospheres

5. SURROUND YOURSELF WITH FEW WELL-CHOSEN ACCESSORIES

Avoid too much plastics or acrylics. Think about an LP cover opposed to a plastic cover for a CD. Candle lights are a must and so is a subtle coloured plaid in pure wool or cashmere. Also consider soft rugs in tonal colours or with smooth patterns.

6. CHOOSE LAMPS FOR ITS PURPOSE AND NOT ONLY ITS DESIGN

Indirect light is great for a hygge atmosphere. Make sure the lamp over your dining table gives sufficient light to 'see' your food and each other. As hygge is also reading a book . when sitting on your sofa surrounded by soft pillows, make sure you have a good reading lamp as well.

7. MUSIC IS A BIG PART OF HYGGE...

...and it must be relaxing. Electronics and their often very hard appearances are hygge killers, so think about storing and hiding electronics with your chosen furniture. For example, a TV cabinet where you can hide the speakers and electronic devices, or a desk where you can close and store your equipment out of sight.

Ways to Master the Danish Art of Hygge in Your Home

Long, dark winter nights and stormy weather have us craving a roaring fire, fluffy slippers, and a soft blanket to curl up under.

As the Danes would say, we want to get hygge. Hygge (pronounced hoo-gah) is the Danish concept of coziness and intimacy—as one tea company puts it, hygge is "taking pleasure from the soothing, ordinary, and inexpensive things in life"—and it has made its way across the Atlantic. To achieve optimal hygge in your own home, grab a warm drink, put on your chunkiest sweater, and check out the below tips.

1. HEAT THINGS UP.

A flickering fire can instantly make any space feel intimate. If you don't have a fireplace in your home, create that warm and cozy vibe by arranging candles of different sizes and shapes into a cluster, says Kayleigh Tanner, owner of the U.K.-based blog Hello Hygge. "My favorites are Yankee Candles in scents like cinnamon and vanilla, but a bag of cheap tea lights will do the trick just as well," Tanner says.

2. BRING THE OUTDOORS INSIDE.

Take a cue from nature (which is innately relaxing and stress-busting) and add some greenery to your home. Can't keep plants alive? Add natural materials like leather, stone, and wood to your space.

3. TURN OFF THE LIGHTS.

Unless you have a dimmer, overhead lights are often too bright to create the homey feeling you're after. So turn off that light and rely on table lamps instead, Tanner says.

4. STREAMLINE.

Cozy spaces might be small, but that doesn't mean they're cluttered. Kate Marengo, founder and president of Interior Chicago, says you can't relax in spaces that are overwhelming. So before you add your hygge touches (candles, a throw, books), take a page from Marie Kondo's book and strip away any extraneous items that don't bring you joy.

5. REACH FOR SOMETHING SOFT.

Texture is a big part of hygge, says Pia Edberg, Vancouver-based author of The Cozy Life. Edberg suggests surrounding yourself with soft items like knitted fleece throw blankets, fluffy pillows, shag rugs, and comfy furniture.

6. SURROUND YOURSELF WITH OBJECTS THAT TELL A STORY.

"There are studies about how hygge in Denmark shies far away from consumerism," Edberg says. Instead of stocking up on mass-produced items, decorate your home with furniture and accents that are meaningful to you. Edberg says this could mean the items were given to you as gifts, you purchased them on your travels, or they are antiques with a rich history

7. KEEP THE HOT DRINKS COMING.

Tanner recommends making your tea kettle your new best friend. She digs Hoogly Tea, a British company that makes hygge their business by selling creative tea blends such as Vanilla Chai, Around the Fire, and Marzipan. Not a tea person? Cocoa or coffee will also do the trick.

8. SET THE TABLE.

Time with family or friends, especially while sharing a great meal, is essential to the hygge philosophy, so you'll need a great dining room table. Danes love a great wooden table and hand-crafted chairs (many will pass down an Arne Jacobsen or a Hans Wegner chair from generation to generation), but any dining room set will do—the important part is spending mealtimes together, says Helen Russell, author of The Year of Living Danishly.

9. SCRUB-A-DUB-DUB, HEAD TO THE TUB.

"Not many people think about the bathroom when they're making their home cozier, but think about making a more relaxing environment for the next time you take a soothing bath," Tanner says. You can do this by lighting a few candles and integrating essential oils and bath products with relaxing scents into your routine. Big, fluffy towels and a quality bathmat are also great additions.

10. GET SMART.

Technology is your secret weapon in making your home cozy, says Carly Pokornowski Moeller, owner and registered interior designer at Unpatterned in Chicago. Wireless speakers can help you use music to set the right mood throughout your home. And, Pokornowski Moeller says, adding a total smart home system (like Nest) can allow you to change the temperature or turn off the lights in any room right from your smartphone. This way you can stop running from room to room to adjust and can just be present.

Creating The Danish Hygge Look At Home

There's no getting away from it, with no less than ten books published on the subject this year, hygge (pronounced 'heurgha') is the new trend everyone is going crazy for. While this 18th-century Danish phenomenon applies to wellness and creating a happier life in general, it is also visually embodied in Danish decor – briefly, it's a cosy, candle-lit sanctuary that's serene, simple and shared with friends and family. Here are 12 inspiring decor ideas to add hygge to your own home for a healthier and happier lifestyle.

Keep it pure and simple

The Dane's aren't ones for embellishment or 'loud' colour schemes – the idea is to create a calm, serene space that is peaceful and free of clutter. Schemes are often purely monochrome, or a subtle mix of harmonious tonal shades.

Light more candles

The Danes light more candles per head than anywhere else in Europe and it's not hard to see why. The warm glow of a candle simply can't be replaced by artificial lighting; it's about creating an inviting atmosphere and developing a soft, kinder form of light that's perfect for relaxing and socialising – two things the Danes do best. Make sure they're white and unscented though, the Danes are purists after all.

Stay in bed

There's nothing better, or more luxurious, than spending an extra hour or two in bed. Luckily, hygge encourages this concept, whether it's enjoying a Sunday doze, reading the morning paper, or having breakfast in bed. Create a cosy space to snuggle up in with plenty of layers – pile on the quilts, blankets and pillows for an indulgent place to relax.

Create a 'hyggekrog', or snug

Every home should have a little cosy nook to retreat to, preferably a window seat with a view looking out to nature. Add layers of cushions and a blanket and enjoy an afternoon of peace and quiet with a good book.

Get a fire going

Huddling around a roaring fire with family and friends is definitely part of the Danish culture – a wood-burning stove is a great energy-efficient option that the Danes would definitely approve of.

Introduce texture

The Danes use a mixture of materials and pattern as a way of adding character and interest to what would otherwise be a relatively minimalist scheme. They tend to introduce plenty of warm, natural materials, such as wood, leather and wool. The overall look still needs to adhere to a tight colour palette, however, to prevent it from clashing or being too distracting.

Get hygge with friends and family

If nothing else, one of the most important concepts of hygge is to get together with close friends and loved ones in a relaxed environment. Think less formal sit-down dinner party and more a get-together over a good bottle of wine, accompanied by hearty comfort food and homemade bakes served in rustic earthenware. Get the look with House of Fraser's Pebble dinnerware, pictured.

Take it outside

While hygge is usually associated with the chillier winter months, that doesn't stop the Danes enjoying the great outdoors. Wrap up warm in faux fur and blankets, gather around a brazier and surround yourselves with lanterns. Finish it off with an indulgent hot chocolate or a mug of mulled wine. Hygge isn't just for winter either; a day spent lingering over a leisurely picnic in the park or a barbecue at home is equally hygge.

Banish clutter

There's a reason Japanese organisation guru Marie Kondo has sold millions of copies of The Life-Changing Magic of Tidying Up – so many of us desire a mess-free home, and none more so than the Danes. To truly embrace hygge, invest in clever storage solutions that can hide away any unwanted visual clutter to create a serene space.

Display treasured memories

Hygge is all about culturing an environment of happiness, so what better way than to put up a creative display of all your favourite family photos, travel paraphernalia, prints and paintings?

Create a spa-style sanctuary

Rather than a rushing for a quick shower in the morning, make sure your bathroom is a place for rest and rejuvenation. The trend for spa-style bathrooms is on the rise with even saunas – a favourite among Scandinavians – becoming more common in bathrooms across the globe. Simple is often best, however, and nothing beats a soak in a steaming hot bath. Invest in candles, fluffy bath robes, clever storage, good lighting and even a sound system to make your experience as relaxing as possible.

Embrace the old and imperfect

The Danes hate waste, so reuse and recycle objects where you can – get creative by upcycling antique pieces of furniture or find a new use of an old item. The good thing about hygge is that nothing has to be perfect; it's more about the sentimentality of an old armchair that used to belong to a family member, for example, than buying lots of brand-new furniture.

HOW TO 'HYGGE' YOUR COSY LOG HOUSE HOLIDAY

The kings of cosy winter life are without question the Scandinavians. They even have a special word for this, which has no real direct translation – "Hygge". Pronounced "Hooga" it loosely means to have a cosy time inside with friends and family whilst the weather is cold and dark outside. Is this the reason why Danes are officially the happiest people in the world? We certainly think so. We discovered this term when we read 'A Year of Living Danishly' by Helen Russell (which we highly recommend) and ever since we love coming in after a long day working around the lake and getting 'Hygge'!

From lighting candles to good food there are lots of things which make the long winter nights actually something we really look forward to now. The best time for hygge is from autumn through to spring, and especially around Christmas, but you can enjoy this cosy living anytime of year really. With lots of wood and Scandinavian design in our cabins and pools of light from carefully positioned lamps our retreats are an ideal place to escape to for a relaxing few days.

So we thought we would list out our top tips for making your luxury log cabin holiday as cosy as possible. Staying in a Scandinavian lodge with a Finnish hot tub you couldn't be in a better place to snuggle up. Whether you are on a romantic escape, a family break, a honeymoon, or a holiday with your friends, everyone loves the warm feeling you get from Hygge.

1. GET IT TOASTY INSIDE

Easy to do with just a few logs on the Clearview woodburner. The gentle crackling of logs and glowing flames does wonders for a relaxing atmosphere.

2. ENJOY SOME HOT TEA WITH A GOOD BOOK

Make a steaming cup of your favorite drink, choose a comfy place in front of the fire and curl up with one of the books from the shelves.

3. COOK UP A SEASONAL WINTER FEAST

Pick cosy, childhood dishes to treat yourself on your luxury escape. A warm porridge with toasted nuts, apple pieces and some dulche de leche is a Danish classic. Check out the below pictured recipe by 'Grød'. They make the holy grail's of porridge. A big roast with all the trimmings is another classic – head to Jessie Smiths butchers for the best meat and The Market Garden for local vegetables. Stop by Hobbs too and pick up some Danish pastries for the afternoons in front of the wood burner. All three are within a minutes walk of each other in Cirencester. Excited for a winter break yet?

4. CREATE CALMING 'POOLS' OF LIGHT WITH SIDE LIGHTS

An interior design trick that really sets the scene.

5. WATCH A CLASSIC

Put your feet up and watch one of those feel good classics. From Billy Elliot to Love Actually – you know the ones.

6. GO FOR A WALK OR TAKE OUT THE ROWING BOAT

An explore around the lake, seeing the nature around you and realizing how secluded your log cabin really is makes coming back into your luxury getaway even more special. Big snuggly coats, hats, scarves and gloves are all compulsory. The chunkier the knitwear the better.

7. LIGHT SOME CANDLES

The warm glow of candlelight adds a calming vibe. Please remember to use safe candles that cannot be knocked over or pose a fire risk!

8. GATHER ROUND THE FIRE PIT

An outdoor fire brings everyone together and wrapped up in snuggly outfit in the winter months is as warming as ever. There is something about a fire that is completely mesmerizing and you can loose hours staring into it, talking about all the big and small things in life. Comfort food like roasted marshmallows and slow cooked bananas with chocolate come into their element here. Check out our welcome pack on arrival for fun games and things to cook on the fire.

9. MAKE SOME GLØGG

Mulled wine is a Danish classic for an evening of coziness.

10. STARGAZE IN THE HOT TUB

Feel the healing effects of using traditional Finnish hot tubs whilst you take in the stars above, the silhouette of the lake edge and the sounds of nearby wildlife. All putting you in a truly zen frame of mind to tip-toe back indoors with.

11. PLAY A BOARD GAME

Reconnecting with those you have escaped with is a big part of the hygge experience. Dropping the technology and gathering around a table is a lovely way to bring everyone together. Check out your cabins board games cupboard for some classics.

12. PUT ON SOME MUSIC

Music really is the food of love so connect to the wifi, pick a moody playlist and let it be the soundtrack to your memorable hygge weekend in the Cotswold's.

The Danish hygge is all about the atmosphere, the people you're with, having a good time and relaxing. All things we think are synonymous with Log House Holidays. So pick who you want to escape with, choose a date, pack some comfy clothes and come and get hygge!

How to create that Danish feeling of 'hygge' around the holidays

If you think about it, the winter holidays — Christmas, Hanukkah, Kwanzaa — are essentially light-filled festivals that fortify us for the long, cold months ahead. And yet we manage to screw them up by stressing over all the shopping, the events, the cooking, the relatives, the preparation, the expectation for everything to be the most wonderful time of the year.

Instead of holiday joy, we have holiday struggle — and that's where hygge comes in

Yes, hygge — that Danish concept everyone's buzzing about this winter. It's pronounced kind of like cougar but with an "H." And it's kind of like coziness, but deeper than that. It's about enjoying simple pleasures — the warmth of friends, curling up with a book, staring out the window at the falling snow.

Somehow, for a lot of people hygge has turned into buying a bunch of sheepskins and oatmeal-colored throws, but what we are not going to do is show you a bunch of stuff you can buy. Hygge is not about that. It's about recognizing the abundance already present in your life and arranging it so you can enjoy it better. It's about feelings of gratitude and simplicity.

So here's a list of tips you can choose from that could give you that feeling. You don't have to do all of them — just pick a couple that resonate most to you.

1. Leave the world behind when you cross your threshold. Have a place where everyone can drop off or hang their things even it that means shoving all the coats in a pile on a closet floor. Change out of your street shoes and into slippers or thick socks. Hell, change into your pajamas. Might as well. Having these little rituals helps you to leave the world outside your door and makes your home feel more like a refuge.

2. Use indirect lighting and candles. Give your overhead lights a break and try using more side table lamps. And all those decorative candles you've set out? Light them in the evening and enjoy their warm glow.

And light that fireplace if you have one, even if only on the weekends.

3. Arrange your living room furniture so people can face each other. Chances are pretty good your family room is arranged with sofas and chairs facing the television, and there's nothing wrong with that. But see if you can turn a chair or two inward to encourage conversation. Keep some pillows or cushions on the floor near the coffee table for someone to plop right down

upon. Do what you can to encourage sitting on the ground more. (This is where wearing removing shoes and wearing slippers helps.)

4. Keep at least one board game out. Playing board games is super-hygge — it's low-tech and convivial. So keep at least one game handy, whichever game and in whatever placement works for your family. Give yourselves one fewer excuse for not playing more games together.

5. Make your home smell yummy. We all know that magical feeling you get when you smell something wonderful baking in the oven, but that's not the only way to create a cozy aroma. When I was younger, my mom used to simmer a pot of spices on the wood-burning stove just for the smell. Here are some other easy ideas for giving your home a comforting scent.

6. Go outside. Go for a walk. Have a snowball fight. When you come indoors, make a point of relishing that feeling of the heat coming back to your cheeks.

7. Set the thermostat lower. Wearing fuzzy slippers and cozy socks, bundling up in a throw — you can't do these hygge things if you've got your thermostat cranked up to tropical levels. Isn't that sort of a form of denial, anyway? See if you

can tap into the distinct pleasures of a slightly chilly home and enjoy a lower heating bill while you're at it.

8. Start a tea ritual. Or a wine ritual. Whatever works. The idea is, you're taking five or more minutes out to slow down, drink something soothing and reflect. For some of us, that sounds impossible — carve out five minutes when, where?!? I'm wondering that myself right now. But I kind of need it, so I'm pledging to start, today.

9. Eat together as a family more. This is another tough one, including for me and my family. Set a goal for December to eat together around the table a certain number of times a week. If you already do this, yay, you! Keep going. For that matter...

10. Invite people over. Hygge isn't about impressive entertaining. But it is about getting together with your favorite people to eat or drink something really simple. Maybe it's just some dumb slow cooker stew or hot chocolate or popcorn. Don't make it fancy; just make it happen.

11. Keep the holiday cooking and baking plans simpler. We're already hitting you with thousands of holiday recipes on SheKnows because it's so much fun. But we're also showering you with shortcuts and hacks to make it all easier. If you're one of those people who finds yourself baking late into the night or

freaking out over the mess and getting the powdered sugar on the cookies just right, maybe set a goal this year to do less. I have done this, and let me tell you: It's amazing. It's so happy-making. You will thank yourself.

12. Enjoy the magic of imperfection. And speaking of getting the powdered sugar right, if you're one of those high-strung perfectionist types — and yes you are, because rule No. 1 of perfectionism is denying you're a perfectionist — try and let go a little. Cultivate an affection for the irregular. Laugh at your mistakes. Imperfection is what connects us all to each other. It's when you stop trying to prove you're better than everyone and accept that you're just as flawed that you open up to the love and spirit of the season. What could be more hygge than that?

Why You Need a Hygge Family Holiday This Year

I'm writing from a cozy spot in front of the fireplace, lanterns glowing nearby. There are soft blankets and pillows scattered around for any impromptu snuggles and storytimes. I've placed as many candles on elevated (aka childproof) surfaces as possible, and I take pleasure even in the act of lighting them. It's as if watching the wick take the flame is evidence of the cozy warmth of the season, proof that home can be one of the best places to be.

As Americans, we've long lived busyness, the myth that the holiday season must come with stress and pressure. But what if the antidote to the hustle and bustle of the holiday season can be found in a little Scandinavian word? What if by pulling on our thickest sweaters and pouring a steaming cup of cocoa, we can embrace something called hygge (pronounced HOO-gah)?

Hygge — the Danish term for a cozy, warm lifestyle and an emphasis on well-being — is embraced throughout Scandinavia. Now it's catching on in the United States. But hygge can be complex to explain. It's about more than cozy things like candles and cocoa, after all.

"Hygge creates a space to stop, slow down and appreciate the simple — and arguably the most important — things in life," says Line Larsen of the Northwest Danish Association, which is based in Seattle. "This is especially valuable in the midst of stressful times."

I think one of the reasons why hygge has become this thing is there are so many anxieties in the world right now about what's going on," says Trine Hahnemann of Denmark, a cook and author of Scandinavian Comfort Food: Embracing the Art of Hygge. "People are not really feeling comfortable with things, and they are stressed out in their lives."

Hahnemann thinks many look to Scandinavia, with its shorter work hours and world-renowned school systems; they figure that the region has things figured out so why not try something like hygge? Of course, Hahnemann notes, the perception isn't always reality.

"I'm not sure they want to know how [many] taxes we pay," she says with a chuckle.

"But that the idea of hygge," she continues, "that [idea of] you have time at home and you light candles and you make tea and coffee and you sit down with your family — [the Danes] really do that still. We are such a home culture still. And I think people are very fascinated and have that dream Banishing busy

Curious if the idea of hygge could be the antidote to the stress and frenzy of the holidays and how to incorporate it into my own life, I reached out to the Nordic Heritage Museum in

Ballard, a historic Seattle neighborhood with strong Scandinavian roots.

I think the way to create 'hyggelige' moments during the holiday season is to slow down and focus on creating unique moments with your friends and family," says executive assistant musuem Kirstine Bendix Knudsen. "The American [holidays] are very mainstream and commercial-oriented. I think the key to more 'hygge' is to celebrate the [holidays] your way: bake a different type of cookie than everybody else, fill your home with nice aromas and candlelight and invite your friends for a nice get together."

This, as you can imagine, is ideal when you've got kids at home. Since hygge has a lot to do with connection, embracing it is likely to create lasting memories and perhaps even inspire family traditions. Plus, embracing hygge is easy to do, says Melissa Bahen, Oregon-based author of Scandinavian Gatherings and blog Lulu the Baker.

"One of our favorite easy traditions — and one that fits in perfectly with the idea of hygge — is to sit down with our kids for just a few minutes each night before bedtime to read a holiday picture book together," she says. "The older kids love it as much as the little ones do ... It's a nice, quiet moment of cozy togetherness during the busy holiday season."

No matter the tradition, by slowing down and spending quality time together you're likely to create an environment that feels safe, secure and loving — exactly what kids crave.

For me, this holiday I want to spend as much time as possible in the kitchen with my family, spinning sugar and butter into a variety of treats. It's not really about the cookies themselves; it's about the time together. It's about balance, making sure that we eat plenty of homecooked meals amid a flurry of parties. It's about the memories, the small things, that will hopefully stay with us because they're connected to a feeling of love.

TOP 5 HYGGE HOLIDAYS

Experience hygge on a cozy holiday with Magnetic North Travel

As the clocks go back and the night draws in we are all looking for ways to beat the winter blues. Despite the dark, cold winters, global reports rank Denmark as the happiest country in the world year after year, so what is the secret to their happiness? Some experts believe that it is all down to hygge, which loosely translates as 'cosiness' and in practice means enjoying the good things in life, loving simple pleasures and being kind to yourself.

Magnetic North Travel is offering a collection of new holidays across Scandinavia that encompass the hygge way of life and will help us to find some cold comfort during the winter.

Best for romantic hygge...stay in the NEW Arctic TreeHouse Hotel, Finland

Opening on 19 November 2016 is Lapland's newest hotel, the stylish Arctic TreeHouse Hotel, located in the Arctic circle near Rovaniemi. Stay in one of just 32 private pod-suites with their Scandi-cool warm wooden interiors. The floor-to-ceiling glass wall offers incredible views of the frosty Finnish forest below and the Aurora Borealis above. Combine with some winter activities including snowmobile safaris, husky mushing and sleigh rides. Read more...

Best for family hygge...Ice-skating in Finland

Get your skates on and enjoy a hyggelig day of family fun ice-skating in Finnish Lakeland, Europe's largest lake district. The lakes form a labyrinth of narrow waterways, islands and isthmuses and during winter, the water freezes and becomes an enormous ice-rink of intertwining paths ready to be explored. In the past, skating from island to island was an essential way for Finns to get around – now it is an enjoyable winter activity. Under the expert guidance of a local skating guide, skaters will be given a skating lesson and then taken out on the trails. Warm up by the roaring fire with a hot chocolate in one of the log cabins at Resort Järvisydän on the shores of Lake Saimaa. Read more...

Best for Christmas hygge...Tivoli Gardens, Copenhagen

Experience some festive hygge at the Tivoli Gardens where thousands of twinkling fairy lights light up the dark skies and transform the area into an authentic winter wonderland. Sip on a warm cup of hot glögg (mulled wine) and feast on smoked sausages, baked apples and roasted nuts. Best buys include hand-crafted wooden stocking fillers and, ideal for keeping warm during the winter, the traditional Faroese jumpers made famous by the city's best-known actress, Sofie Gråbøl, the star of The Killing. Decorating your home with ornaments is big part of Danish Christmas hygge so why not boost the hygge levels and design your own at Tivoli Gardens – a perfect gift to give. A three-night stay (BB) at the five-star boutique Hotel

Nimb costs from £895pp with flights and transfers included. Enquire

Best for adventure hygge...star-gazing and polar-camping in Spitsbergen

Spend a night under the stars wild camping in the polar wilderness on this three-night trip to Spitsbergen. The first and last nights are spent at Basecamp Trappers Hotel before navigating to the polar camp under the moonlight. The remoteness of the camp provides optimum viewing for the stars and Northern Lights. The tents include a modern heating system to make camp life in the Arctic more comfortable. Telescopes are provided and knowledgeable guides are on hand to give guidance to guests. This new three-night star gazing package costs from £1,245pp and includes flights, airport transfers in Longyearbyen, the Star Gazing Camp excursion (with one night in the polar camp) and two-night's accommodation at Basecamp Trappers Hotel (BB). Enquire

Best for wellbeing hygge...NEW Arctic Yoga Retreat (yoga-on-ice) under the Northern Lights

Wanderlusting yogis looking to perfect their downward dog, restore their wellbeing and connect with their surroundings should consider the new Arctic Winter Yoga Retreat. Located deep within the Arctic Circle near Jokkmokk in Swedish Lapland this snow and ice yoga retreat takes place 23-26 March, 2017 at the Aurora Safari Camp - a pop-up camp consisting of traditional Sami Lavvu (similar to a tepee), and located in the wilderness, far away from any light pollution, on the frozen Råne River. The retreat offers guests daily virya yoga classes, which take place on the ice-covered river and in the lavvu. The winter wonderland scenery and Arctic silence combined with the guided meditation classes will take guests on a journey of inner self discovery. Accommodation is in traditional style Sami Lavvu at the Aurora Safari Camp. The modern day version features lots of home comforts including a wood-burning stove. The ice camp also features a wood-fired sauna and icy plunge pool ideal for getting the heart pumping and the blood circulating as well as relaxing muscles.

Embracing "hygge" in the workplace

Hygge (pronounced hoo-gah), the Danish concept taking the US by storm, is characterized as making ordinary, every day moments more meaningful, or being aware and taking pleasure in a good moment, whether simple or special. While there's no direct translation to English, many compare it mindfulness, or a feeling of coziness and contentedness. Since the Danes are reportedly the happiest people on earth, maybe embracing hygge in our lives and at work in particular, might do us all some good, and even boost our productivity.

Here are four ways to hygge at the office:

1.Personalize the open plan | Many companies are implementing open plan offices, which are great for cross-collaboration and intra-office communication. However, depending on the type of work being done, it can seem either jarringly quiet or distractingly loud. An area rug can help dampen sound but can also help create the cozy, authentic and inspiring spaces people crave. Another great way to combat these extremes is to implement acoustic solutions. White noise can be comforting and help improve productivity, so adding sound masking, like the QtPro by Steelcase, works to decrease distractions and improve speech privacy.

2.Find a cozy spot | If your office is open-concept, finding a space that feels more intimate can help you to feel more inspired and productive. Privacy is a real necessity in the workplace so offering solutions where people can focus, recharge and do head's down work is imperative. The Brody WorkLounge by Steelcase is a high-performing and comfortable workspace that provides privacy and shelter from visual distractions. It's a smart alternative to enclaves and transforms under-utilized spaces into desirable destinations.

3.Make time for lunch | Taking a lunch break is good for all aspects of our health. If you have a WorkCafé or cafeteria, eat your lunch there instead of at your desk. Socializing with coworkers and making personal connections benefits your overall enjoyment while at work and allows you to re-energize for afternoon productivity. Sitting all day in the same position isn't great for your physical health so getting up from your desk during lunch also provides a change in posture.

4.Rethink meetings | Meetings are essential, but to make them more intimate and productive, schedule smaller meetings when possible. Fewer participants can yield richer and more meaningful conversations, with increased opportunity for people to participate and express ideas. Huddle rooms offer versatility and functionality better suited to these types of meetings—smaller tables and sitting closer to colleagues promotes working as a cohesive team. If a meeting isn't dependent on conferencing technology, informal lounge areas and the WorkCafé can be inspiring and collaborative spaces.

Yes, these can all be considered general best practices for wellbeing in the office, but viewing them through a hygge lens reminds us why they are such an important focus in the workplace. As we strive for a work/life balance, our time at work should feel productive, enjoyable and fulfilling.

Ways to use Hygge to Get Cozy At Work

Hygge is coziness and well-being. Hygge is creating a space that feels welcoming, warm and comfy. Hygge is enjoying and valuing the small things in life—like intimate conversations with friends and family over a big bowl of porridge.

But why is hygge important to the Danes? There is relatively little daylight in Denmark during the winter, so to compensate for the cold and dark, their hygge dial is cranked up to eleven ("top hygge"). And while this term has been received into American culture with a little bit of side-eye and skepticism, I'll sign onto whatever gets more hot cocoa into my life.

In fact, I have told anyone who'll listen that hygge is my goal for this winter. At home, my husband, daughter and I create hygge by snuggling under blankets, building a fire in the fireplace, turning down the lamps and drinking hot beverages. We put on fuzzy robes and spend too much time reading, sitting too close to the radiators. And this is great for weekends, but how can we bring hygge to work—when we're inside missing all the good daylight?

As designers, we are more likely to be attuned and affected by the spaces around us. We are more likely to be observant, see what works, test things out to make things better. So can we be user experiences experts for ourselves, and try to infuse a little hygge into work?

Upgrade your desk

There are some obvious changes that can makes your own space feel cozier, presuming they don't break the fire code and don't tick off your cubemates:

1.Add a lamp with an incandescent bulb to counteract the overhead fluorescents and the blue light coming from your screen.

2.Keep a cushy scarf or jacket on the back of your chair to combat cool office temps and stiff chairs. Better yet, put that scarf/jacket on your lap as a makeshift blanket.

3.Switch shoes (or don't). I'd venture a guess that nobody would notice if you "forgot" to change out of your commuting sneakers/winter boots.

4.Try some noise. Sure, I work for NPR, but I can't listen to music, radio or podcasts and concentrate on design at the same time (oh, the irony). But there is something to the idea that white noise of various forms—like my favorite, brown noise—can be comforting. Colleagues also like white noise that sounds like a coffee shop.

Find a cozy spot

1.If you have a supportive office who trusts that you will work even when you're not at your desk, try some alternate spaces for a change of scene.

2.If your office is open-concept and spacious, find or make a space that feels more intimate. Drag a comfy chair next to a bookcase, or see if there's a small room or office where you might work from time to time.

Change meeting locations. If you're not dependent on conference room technology, convene the team in the common area or cafe. Find smaller tables and sit closer to your colleagues.

Make little chats a regular thing

Personal connection is an aspect of hygge that I both desire and fear. I'm an introvert who thinks other people are really interesting, so I often want to talk — but feel anxious about it.

1. Schedule brief weekly check-ins with your favorite coworkers to make sure you continue to connect, even when things get busy. These folks are your gut check/cheerleader/commiserator.

2. For a colleague you'd like to know better, invite them to a 30-minute one-on-one. This can be a quick coffee, Skype chat or lunchroom catch-up. You don't need an agenda, but do consider a few things to keep up conversation.

3. Don't forget about colleagues who work remotely! They may need help making and maintaining personal connections, so be a pal and reach out.

Get more daylight

You may like the extra sun in the morning, or despise commuting home in the dark. But November means the end of Daylight Saving Time, and we are stuck with it until the spring. We can avoid "falling back" into a funk by setting more time aside for daylight.

1. I know everyone says to leave your desk at lunch, and I wish I took their advice. I am much more likely to walk away during that hour if I have an errand, so think up a few little chores you can do near the office that will get you outside.

2. Consider small adjustments to your commute to get a little daylight. Leave the train one stop earlier. Walk to the second-closest bus stop. Park just a little further away.

3. Take smoke breaks. No, I'm totally kidding! But if your day is flexible, consider walking to grab a (third) coffee or simply do a lap around the block.

"But wait," you might say.

Aren't these suggestions just general good practices for a better work environment? Well, yes. You caught me. But adding the framing of hygge can help focus our efforts on ways to combat the cold, dark months of winter while keeping our work-selves just as happy and healthy as our home-selves.

Designers are specially equipped to see where small changes can be made to a larger effect, and we can communicate the importance of those changes to the folks around us. So why not be hygge ambassadors at work?

Conclusions to Denmark's Happiness

1. Simple commute

It might be long, but at least it's not complicated! The Danish transportation system is very modern and efficient. If you're not within walking or biking distance of a train station, you can easily hop on a bus to get to your destination; the bus stops are everywhere! The train makes your commute even easier, as you can bring your bike on board for free.

Even though fellow DIS Blogger Carli has a long commute, she makes the most of her time on the train—check out her thoughts here. Maybe Danes are such a happy people because, instead of spending their time sitting in traffic on their morning commute, they are able to relax in one of Denmark's comfortable public transportation vehicles.

DIS Blogger Bailey, who is in the Urban Studies program at DIS, has learned about the intricacies of the public transportation system in Denmark—take a look at her insightful thoughts in her post!

2. Pedestrian-friendly streets

It's nice not to have to share your path to class with tons of buses and cars. Just watch out for the bikes! Not only are the streets as cute as you could imagine, but the fact that you're not constantly watching out for loud cars zooming by makes your walk to and from classes much more enjoyable. DIS is located in a perfect area for students—a few steps from restaurants, bakeries, and cozy cafes!

3. Pastries everywhere!

From Danish birthday parties to mid-week pick-me-ups, indulging in warm, freshly baked pastries is easy when bakeries are on every corner in Copenhagen. On Wednesdays, many bakeries sell specific cinnamon rolls, or snegles as they call them. They're so popular, sometimes there is a line out the door!

4. Cute kids in even cuter snowsuits

While many people assume that cold weather makes people unhappy, Danes manage to stay positive throughout the winter season, and I think it's mostly because their kids are so precious! Everywhere you look during the winter months, you see these tiny humans dressed in the tiniest snowsuits. On my short study tour with my Children in a Multicultural Context course, I was able to visit a Forest Kindergarten. There, all of the kids were covered in head to toe. Plus, these outfits keep the kids so warm they can fall in ice-cold puddles and not even bat an eye. Danes let their children learn from experience, which is perhaps another reason for their 'happiest country' title—they aren't constantly worried about the safety of their kids.

5. Hygge

After a few months here, I think I've finally grasped the concept. You see, hygge isn't a word—it's a feeling. It's that feeling you get when you come inside after a long, cold, windy day and see your host has finished making dinner and the whole house smells like frikadeller. It's the warmth of a few candles at the coffee shop to help you get through studying for that midterm. It's when your host dog jumps on your bed and refuses to leave until you rub his belly and cuddle him. Hygge is what makes Denmark feel like home.

6. The feeling of (sort of) understanding another language

Let's be real: Danish is sometimes a strange language. It has been a struggle to learn when I'm 20 and have lost most ability to learn unique phonemes. Even though most Copenhageners speak English, train station names and signs are in Danish. After four months of living in Denmark and taking my Danish Language and Culture class, I finally feel that I am not as utterly confused as when I first got here. (but – I am still trying to figure out how 'æ' sounds any different than 'a'!)

7. Casual fashion

Locals have perfected the 'effortless' style, so you'll never feel underdressed walking the streets of Copenhagen. While you won't see too many people wearing workout clothes – Danes still manage to look put together without dressing too fancy. The mentality when putting together an outfit seems to be based on practicality; sneakers are often paired with skirts or dresses, and clothes are professional but not stiff! If you want to know what your clothes mean in Scandinavia, consider enrolling in The Meaning of Style at DIS.

Whether in a suburb or right in the heart of Copenhagen, you are never far from some kind of nature. Because the city is located along the shore, water is all around you. If you ever need a break from the stress of school or life in general, a quick bike ride to the beach will calm your thoughts. And trust me, the beach is just as amazing (if not more) in the winter.

Made in the USA
San Bernardino, CA
08 December 2018